SIMPSONS™

COMICS

COLOSSAL COMPENDIUM
VOLUME FIVE

TITAN BOOKS

SIMPSONS COMICS COLOSSAL COMPENDIUM
VOLUME FIVE

Materials previously published in
Bart Simpson #85, Kang & Kodos #1, The Malevolent Mr. Burns #1, Professor Frink #1,
Ralph Wiggum Comics #1, Simpsons Comics #208, #210, #220,
Simpsons Summer Shindig #8, #9, Simpsons Super Spectacular #7, #15

Published in the UK by Titan Books, a division of Titan Publishing Group Ltd.,
144 Southwark St., London SE1 0UP, under licence from Bongo Entertainment, Inc.

FIRST EDITION: JULY 2017

ISBN 9781783296569

2 4 6 8 10 9 7 5 3 1

Publisher: Matt Groening

Creative Director: Nathan Kane
Managing Editor: Terry Delegeane
Director of Operations: Robert Zaugh
Art Director: Jason Ho
Assistant Art Director: Mike Rote
Production Manager: Christopher Ungar
Assistant Editor: Karen Bates
Production: Art Villanueva
Administration: Ruth Waytz
Legal Guardian: Susan A. Grode

Printed by TC Transcontinental, Beauceville, QC, Canada. 05/15/17

D'OH-LICE ACADEMY

MAX DAVISON
WRITER

PHIL ORTIZ
PENCILS

MIKE DECARLO
INKS

ART VILLANUEVA
COLORS

KAREN BATES
LETTERS

NATHAN KANE
EDITOR

MR. *HURLBUT*?! FROM THE SPRINGFIELD HISTORICAL SOCIETY?

WHAT ARE YOU DOING HERE?

CONGRATULATING MR. *SIMPSON*, CHIEF. YOU SEE, HE HAS JUST BROKEN A *HUNDRED-YEAR-OLD* RECORD!

I DID?

YES. WHILE IN THAT TANK, YOU HELD YOUR BREATH FOR *SEVEN MINUTES AND ONE SECOND!*

WONDERFUL. CAN I ARREST HIM NOW?

MR. SIMPSON'S FEAT IS QUITE HISTORIC.

ARE YOU FAMILIAR WITH *OBADIAH "CHEEKS" WILMINGTON*?

WAS HE THE LEAD SINGER FOR BLUES TRAVELER?

"BACK IN 1889, LAZY POLICE CHIEF OBADIAH WILMINGTON HAD HIS AUTHORITY CHALLENGED BY AMBROSE ROLLINS."

"OBADIAH KNEW HE WOULD LOSE IN AN ELECTION. SO THE CHIEF, WHO HAD THE *BIGGEST CHEEKS IN TOWN*, PROPOSED A DIFFERENT COMPETITION..."

"WHOEVER COULD HOLD THEIR BREATH THE LONGEST WOULD WEAR THE BADGE!"

"OBADIAH EASILY WON THE COMPETITION, HOLDING HIS BREATH FOR EXACTLY *SEVEN* MINUTES."

"A FEAT THAT HAS NEVER BEEN REPEATED. UNTIL *NOW*."

TO PROTECT HIS POWER, CHIEF WILMINGTON ADDED A NEW LAW TO THE TOWN CHARTER. STATUTE 19A, SUBPARAGRAPH C, LINE 221...

"WHOSOEVER HOLDS HIS BREATH FOR OVER SEVEN MINUTES, SHALL BE NAMED THE SPRINGFIELD *CHIEF OF POLICE*."

BUT THIS MEANS...YOU CAN'T...

SO YOU'RE SAYING...I'M THE *NEW CHIEF*?

WAY TO GO, HOMER! NOW, THERE ARE A COUPLE THINGS I'D LIKE YOU TO TURN A *BLIND EYE* TO...

:SIGH!: I DON'T KNOW WHO I *AM* WITHOUT THAT BADGE! BEING CHIEF WAS MY CALLING!

IF ONLY I CAN FIND ANOTHER JOB THAT REQUIRES THE SAME LEVEL OF LAZINESS AND LACK OF AMBITION...

SOON...

DO YOU HAVE ANY EXPERIENCE WITH SAFETY?

WELL, I WAS SPRINGFIELD'S CHIEF OF POLICE FOR OVER A DECADE. DOES THAT COUNT?

JUDGING FROM OUR HIGH CRIME RATE, I'M GOING TO SAY "NO." UNFORTUNATELY, THE ONLY OTHER APPLICANT WAS DISCO STU...

RADIATION IS SWEEPING THE NATION!

YOU MAY NOT BE MR. RIGHT, BUT YOU'RE MR. *RIGHT NOW!* WELCOME TO SECTOR 7G, CLANCY.

YAY?

YOU'LL FIND THE *DONUTS* OVER THERE.

I MEAN, *"YAY!"*

MEANWHILE...

WEE-OOO! WEE-OOO!

THAT'S THE NEW SIREN I INSTALLED! WE GOTTA MOVE!

MCBAIN, YOU DRIVE!

BUT, CHIEF, I'M NOT A VERY GOOD DRIVER--

I DON'T WANT TO HEAR IT, MCBAIN! SHUT UP AND DRIVE!

WHOA!

HURRY! WE CAN'T LET THIS GET AWAY FROM US!

SKREECH!

SKID!

SWERVE!

RINGFIELD ELEMENTARY SCHOOL

POLI

SPD 1

HUFF! TELL ME I'M NOT TOO LATE!

IT'S 10:59 A.M. WE'RE STILL SERVING BREAKFAST.

WOO-HOO! THAT MAGIC TIME BEFORE HASH BROWNS TURN INTO FRENCH FRIES!

GREAT WORK, SIMPSON!

HUH? BUT YOU JUST SAID I WAS LAZY AND TERRIBLE!

AND THAT'S *EXACTLY WHAT WE EXPECT* FROM OUR POLICE CHIEF.

WHEN YOU FIRST GOT THE JOB, WE ASSUMED THE CITY WOULD BE ON FIRE WITHIN 48 HOURS. ANYTHING LESS IS A BONUS!

AW...I THOUGHT I WAS DOING A *GOOD* "GOOD JOB"!

YOU ARE! HAVE ANOTHER COPPER CRULLER!

WELL, OKAY, BUT I WON'T ENJOY IT... MUCH.

THAT NIGHT...

I'M A FAILURE! AND THE WHOLE TOWN KNOWS IT!

...AND THIS IS NEWS?

LISA, AREN'T YOU GOING TO TELL DADDY THAT HE SQUANDERED HIS CHANCE TO ENACT SERIOUS SOCIAL CHANGE?

ACTUALLY, I'VE BECOME INDIFFERENT. I'VE ACCEPTED THAT THE *STATUS QUO* IS WHAT IT IS.

NO! I DON'T WANT MY LITTLE GIRL TO BE *INDIFFERENT*! I WANT HER TO BURN WITH THE INTENSITY OF A MILLION WHITE-HOT SUNS! MY COURSE IS CLEAR!

THE NEXT DAY...

FROM NOW ON I'M TAKING THIS JOB SERIOUSLY. I CLEARED OUT THE DEADWEIGHT AND BROUGHT IN PEOPLE THAT I CAN TRUST!

LENNY AND CARL, WELCOME TO THE FORCE!

POLICE CHIEF

WE'RE GOING TO MAKE SOME SERIOUS CHANGE AROUND HERE!

BUT WE'RE STILL KEEPING THE *SHORTS*, RIGHT?

WELL *DUH*, LENNY! I'M NOT CRAZY!

WE'RE GOING TO ROOT OUT ALL THE CRIMINALS IN SPRINGFIELD! WE'LL SEARCH EVERY WAREHOUSE, ROADHOUSE, DOGHOUSE, STEAKHOUSE...

MMM.... STEAKHOUSE...

ALL RIGHT! TIME TO CLEAN UP THIS CITY!

LET'S TAKE CARE OF SOME...*FAMILY* BUSINESS.

WHERE DO WE START?

KRR-ACK!

MEANWHILE...

CHARLIE, WATCH OUT!

THAT LADDER ISN'T SECURE! MAKE SURE YOU'VE GOT SOMEONE HOLDING IT!

GEE, THANKS!

I'VE GOT TO SAY, CLANCY, THERE HAVE BEEN *NO ACCIDENTS* SINCE YOU'VE TAKEN OVER! NICE WORK!

I GUESS I'M FINALLY MOTIVATED!

UNLIKE BEING POLICE CHIEF, A SAFETY INSPECTOR *CAN* ACTUALLY MAKE A DIFFERENCE!

ANGER

YOU'RE DOING A GREAT JOB, CHIEF!

"CHIEF." AH...THAT TAKES ME BACK!

ACROSS TOWN...

THE POLICE REUNION CONCERT ONE NIGHT ONLY!

I AM, LIKE, SO STOKED FOR THIS! STEALING THIS CONCERT TICKET WAS THE BEST DECISION OF MY LIFE!

WELL, I GUESS THIS TOWN MIGHT BE SAFER WITH YOU IN CHARGE, WIGGY.

JUST PROMISE NOT TO WORK TOO HARD.

EASIEST PROMISE I EVER MADE!

EMPLOYEE LOUNGE

BUT, CHIEF! THE PLANT HAS NEVER BEEN SAFER! YOU CAN'T JUST WALK AWAY!

SORRY, MR. SMITHERS. IF THERE'S ONE THING I'VE LEARNED, IT'S THAT YOU CAN'T ARGUE WITH AN ARCHAIC STATUTE FROM THE TOWN CHARTER.

LATER...

AH...IT'S GREAT TO BE BACK. IT'S HIGH TIME I MAKE SOME SERIOUS CHANGES TO THE POLICE FORCE!

FIRST OFF, WE'RE GETTING THAT STUPID BREATH HOLDING LAW OFF THE BOOKS!

NOW, FOR THE *IMPORTANT* BUSINESS. DO WE HAVE ANY COPPER CRULLERS LEFT?

SORRY, CHIEF. HOMER ATE THE LAST BOX.

DONUTS

GRRR! THERE OUGHTA BE A *LAW*...

THE END

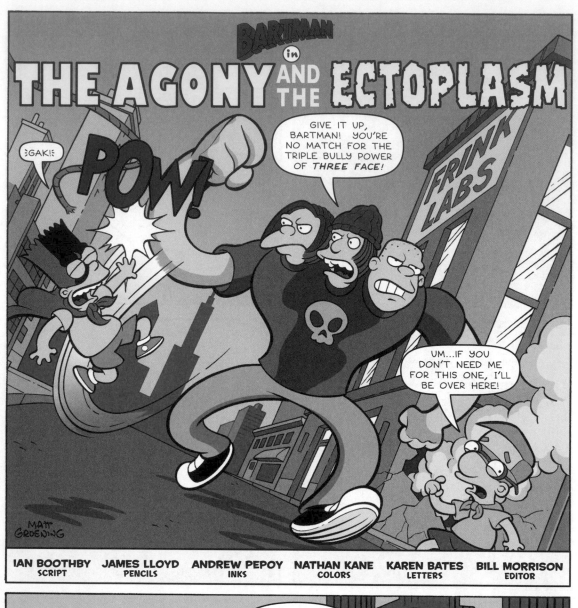

BARTMAN in

THE AGONY AND THE ECTOPLASM

:GAK!:

POW!

GIVE IT UP, BARTMAN! YOU'RE NO MATCH FOR THE TRIPLE BULLY POWER OF *THREE FACE*!

FRINK LABS

UM...IF YOU DON'T NEED ME FOR THIS ONE, I'LL BE OVER HERE!

MATT GROENING

IAN BOOTHBY	**JAMES LLOYD**	**ANDREW PEPOY**	**NATHAN KANE**	**KAREN BATES**	**BILL MORRISON**
SCRIPT	PENCILS	INKS	COLORS	LETTERS	EDITOR

WHAT HAPPENED, PROFESSOR?

THESE THREE LADS WERE HELPING ME OUT AS PART OF THEIR COURT-ORDERED COMMUNITY SERVICE WORK WHEN SOMETHING WENT ALL :FLOYVEN!:

¡MOOOOAN!¡

WE **DID** IT! WE BEAT THREE FACE!

WE SURE DID BEAT HIM! WE GAVE HIM THE OL' *ONE-TWO-SKIDOO!*

EVIL BETTER BEWARE OF THE TERRIFIC TRIO! BARTMAN, HOUSE-BOY, AND SALESMAN!

THE THING IS...WE'RE MORE OF A *DYNAMIC DUO*. FRANKLY, I THINK EVEN HAVING ONE PARTNER IS ONE TOO MANY SOMETIMES!

HEY!

NOW BEFORE YOU SLAM THE DOOR IN OL' GIL'S FACE, LEMME SHOW YOU MY STUFF! I'VE GOT *THE GOODS!*

LOOK HERE! I MADE MY OWN *SWINGING ROPE* USING LAWN DARTS THAT WERE BANNED YEARS AGO!

SALESMAN *AWAY!*

BUT *THIS* IS THE TALLEST BUILDING AROUND HERE. WHAT IS IT *ATTACHED* TO?

NOTHING APPARENTLY!

THUD!

AND SO WE LAY TO REST BELOVED CITIZEN AND LOVABLE LOSER *GIL GUNDERSON*.

IT WAS NICE OF YOU TO COME PAY YOUR RESPECTS, MRS. SKINNER.

RESPECTS NOTHING! HE STILL OWES ME FOR A BROKEN JUICER HE SOLD ME IN THE NINETIES. I'M GONNA GO THROUGH HIS POCKETS BEFORE YOU PUT HIM IN THE GROUND!

IT'S NOT YOUR FAULT, BART. IF YOU HAVE TO BLAME ANYONE, BLAME THE GUY WHO INVENTED GRAVITY!

I JUST FEEL I COULD HAVE DONE SOMETHING MORE FOR HIM.

I WISH I HAD A CHANCE TO SAY...

SAY WHAT?

I DON'T KNOW. MAYBE SAY I SHOULD HAVE GIVEN HIM A CHANCE.

WAIT A SECOND! *GIL!* YOU'RE A G-G-*GHOST!*

THAT'S RIGHT! I'M A GHOST NOW.

IF YOU REALLY WANT TO GIVE ME ANOTHER CHANCE, MAYBE I'LL DO BETTER LIKE THIS!

LATER, BACK AT FRINK'S LAB...

SO NELSON WAS DOING COMMUNITY SERVICE WHEN HE DRANK ONE OF MY FORMULAS, THINKING IT WAS SODA POP! GA-HOY!

AND NOW I CAN *TURN INTO* SODA! NOTHING CAN STOP *THE FIZZ!* HAW HAW!

SPLASH!

CAN YOU JUST STOP LETTING BULLIES WORK HERE?

HE'S TRASHING MY LAB AND MAKING THE MONKEY'S BURP, WHICH IS SO *STINKY* WITH ALL THE *BANANAS* AND THE *WHATNOT!*

BRAAAAP!

BLAAAARP!

SMASH!

HEYA, PARTNER! SORRY I'M LATE, BUT I--

HA! HA! THAT'S FUNNY!

WHAT?

YOU'RE LATE BECAUSE YOU'RE DEAD. GA-HEY! YOU'RE THE LATE GIL!

STILL DON'T FOLLOW YOU.

YOU SEE...

HEY, GUYS!

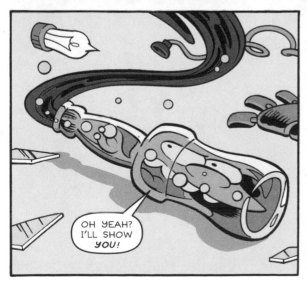

YOU'RE NOT GOING TO EAT MY *BRAIN*, ARE YOU?

NO, I HAD A BIG LUNCH. BUT NOW I HAVE NOWHERE TO GO AND NOTHING TO MY NAME EXCEPT MY CASE OF OLD SUPERHERO GADGETS.

GIL, I THINK I HAVE AN IDEA...

AND SO...

AND YOU SAY THIS IS A *TOP OF THE LINE* SPRING-LOADED, BOXING GLOVE BAZOOKA?

YOU HAVE OL' GIL'S STAMP OF QUALITY!

AND SO AGAIN...

ALL RIGHT, SPRINGFIELD CREDIT UNION, THIS IS A STICK UP! HAND OVER THE CASH, OR I'LL *MIKE TYSON* YOU!

YOU MEAN YOU'LL BITE OFF OUR EARS?

WELL, IF IT ISN'T THE RETURN OF THE SUPER DUDES, OR SHOULD I SAY SUPER *DUDS!*

TIME TO BOX YOUR EARS, KIDDOS!

LIKE...*OW!*

POW!

SPROING!

THE END

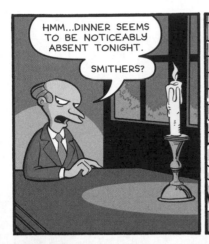

HMM...DINNER SEEMS TO BE NOTICEABLY ABSENT TONIGHT.

SMITHERS?

RIGOROUS BATHTIME EXFOLIATIONS AREN'T FORTHCOMING.

SMITHERS?

:TCCH!: THE HOUNDS AREN'T GOING TO RELEASE *THEMSELVES!*

SMIIITHERRRRS!

WOO!

WOOOO!

MR. BURNS TO THE RESCUE

NATHAN KANE
SCRIPT

TONE RODRIGUEZ
PENCILS

ANDREW PEPOY
INKS

ART VILLANUEVA
COLORS

KAREN BATES
LETTERS

BOTHERATION! WHERE THE DEUCE COULD THAT SCULLION HAVE RUN OFF TO? I HAVE A MIND TO GIVE HIM THE *CASTIGATION* OF A LIFETIME!

PERHAPS IT'S TIME TO USE MY FABLED ABILITY OF *TOTAL RECALL...*

MATT GROENING

HMMMM...

HMMMM...

HUZZAH! THAT'S IT! I REMEMBER IT AS IF IT WAS YESTERDAY!

YESTERDAY...

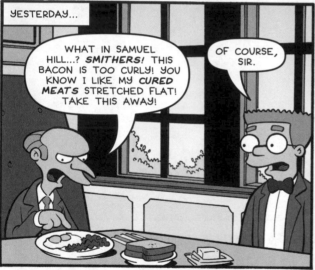

WHAT IN SAMUEL HILL...? *SMITHERS!* THIS BACON IS TOO CURLY! YOU KNOW I LIKE MY *CURED MEATS* STRETCHED FLAT! TAKE THIS AWAY!

OF COURSE, SIR.

GO DOWN TO THE BASEMENT AND FETCH MY *LEFT-HANDED BACON STRETCHER!* YOU CAN USE IT TO RE-PREPARE THIS TRAVESTY YOU CALL BREAKFAST.

¡CHUCKLE!¿

CEASE YOUR CACOPHONOUS *GIGGLES AND GUFFAWS,* YOU LACKWIT! DID I SAY SOMETHING HUMOROUS?

WELL... ER...

NO, SIR. IT'S JUST THAT...A LEFT-HANDED BACON STRETCHER DOESN'T ACTUALLY EXIST. WHEN I WAS A BOY AT CAMP, WE USED TO SEND THE YOUNGER KIDS OUT LOOKING FOR ONE AS A JOKE. KIND OF LIKE A *SNIPE HUNT*...YOU KNOW, A FOOL'S ERRAND.

ONE SUMMER DAY IN SPRINGFIELD...

THE *SUN!* WHAT HAPPENED TO THE *SUN?*

UP *THERE*...!

WHAT *IS* THAT?

SPRINGFIELD COMMUNITY POOL
(ONE DIP GIVES YOU YOUR YEARLY DOSE OF CHLORINE.)

CANNONBAALLL!

POOLIN' AROUND

MATT GROENING

MIKE W. BARR SCRIPT   **REX LINDSEY** PENCILS   **DAN DAVIS** INKS   **NATHAN HAMILL** COLORS   **KAREN BATES** LETTERS   **NATHAN KANE** EDITOR

NEARBY...

I'D JUST LIKE TO...ER, AH... THANK YOU ALL FOR ATTENDING THIS MAYORAL FUNDRAISER...

RE-ELECT "DIAMOND JOE" QUIMBY

...AND I'D APPRECIATE IT IF YOU'D *DONATE* TO MY CAMPAIGN THE SAME WAY YOU *VOTE*...*EARLY* AND *OFTEN!*

HA! HA! HA!

SPA-LOOSH!

WHOOSH!

GOOD LORD!

"DIA

RE-ELECT "DIAMOND JOE" QUIMBY

ONE SIDE! OUT OF MY...ER, AH...WAY!

VOTE QUIMBY!

SPLOOSH!

MY CHECKS!

WELL, THIS CERTAINLY WON'T BE THE FIRST TIME I'VE LAUNDERED MY CONTRIBUTIONS.

THANK YOU ALL FOR ATTENDING... LET'S DO THIS AGAIN, SOON!

GOOD JOB, HOMER! YOU TAUGHT ME THAT HOLLYWOOD IS *WRONG*...A GIANT ASTEROID *WOULDN'T* WIPE OUT THE EARTH!

SHUT UP, BOY!

SIMPSON! I SHOULD HAVE *KNOWN* YOU WERE BEHIND THIS DELUGE OF BIBLICAL PROPORTIONS!

THE WHO DID THE WHAT NOW?

I'D HAVE YOU *ARRESTED*, BUT WIGGUM AND HIS KEYSTONE KOPS ARE EVEN MORE INCOMPETENT THAN *YOU!*

SO INSTEAD, I'M *CANCELING* THE POOL'S BUDGET FOR THE REST OF THE SUMMER!

HUH?

THE NEXT MORNING...

OKAY, SPRINGFIELD! LET'S HIT THE POOL *SIMPSONS-STYLE!*

OOPS!

HA! LOOKS LIKE YOUR SWIM TRUNKS JUST LOST THE BATTLE OF THE *BULGE!*

FLAPT!

WHY, YOU LITTLE--!

¡GAK!¿

BEEP!
BEEP!

HIYA, HOMER! ¿URP!¿ WHERE DO YA WANT ALL THIS *SAND?*

BARNEY! RIGHT ON TIME! JUST POUR IT OUT AROUND THE POOL!

GREAT IDEA, HUH? THE SAND WILL GIVE US THAT "BEACH" ATMOSPHERE! PEOPLE *LOVE* SAND!

NOT JUST *PEOPLE,* DAD...!

SAND KING

YARRGH! GLOOOOK!

...SO DO *CATS!*

MEOW!

MROW!

WELL, NO WORRIES! PEOPLE *LIKE* CATS!

DAD, I DON'T THINK YOU'RE THINKING THIS THROUGH.

NO TIME, LISA! YOU TALK SOME *SENSE* INTO THOSE CATS! *I'VE* GOT ANOTHER IDEA!

BUT YOU *CAN'T* TALK SENSE INTO CATS!

OH, DEAR...

WHAT'S THE *MATTER*, MOM? THIS ISN'T *TOO* BAD.

NOT YET, BUT WHEN YOUR FATHER SAYS HE HAS "AN IDEA"...THAT'S *NEVER* GOOD!

AND *SOMEONE* NEEDS TO KEEP THE OTHER CHILDREN OCCUPIED.

WHAT DO YOU THINK MOM HAS IN MIND?

NO IDEA. BUT UNLIKE DAD, AT LEAST SHE'S *GOT* A MIND!

SOMETIME LATER...

?

WOW, MOM! THIS *IS* A GOOD IDEA...!

BUILD YOUR DREAM SAND CASTLE

NO, SWEETIE, YOU'RE DOING IT WRONG. DO IT LIKE *THIS*!

...I *THINK*. I FORGOT JUST HOW PARTICULAR SHE CAN BE.

HERE, MAGGIE, LET ME *HELP* YOU--!

ALL RIGHT, ALL *RIGHT*!

PAF!

SHEESH, WHAT'S GOTTEN INTO *HER*?

THE FOUNTAIN HEAD

HEY! NO *SAND THROWING*!

DAD? WHAT ARE YOU *DOING*?

SORRY, HONEY! DADDY WANTED TO SHOW YOU HIS LATEST *FIND*!

ARE YOU ALL RIGHT?

NOT... YET...

I NEED MOUTH-TO-MOUTH!

HRMMM...

OH, YOU'RE FINE!

CAN'T BLAME A GUY FOR TRYING!

COME ON! LET'S PRETEND WE'RE PIRATES!

CORPORATE OR POLITICAL?

9FT

YEARGH!

TOSS!

EEK! A CAT ON THE RAFT!

HSSS!

THAT'S MY LEAST FAVORITE DR. SEUSS BOOK!

KA-POP!

THE BIG KANG THEORY!

MATT GROENING

IAN BOOTHBY
WRITER

JACOB CHABOT
ART

ART VILLANUEVA
COLORS

KAREN BATES
LETTERS

NATHAN KANE
EDITOR

*LIKE AN EARTH SIGH BUT, Y'KNOW, IN SPACE. – EDITOR NATHAN

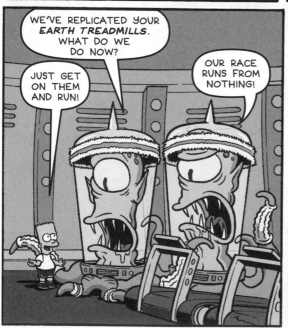

AND SO...

THAT DOES IT! IT'S NO USE! I'LL NEVER GET BACK IN SHAPE!

I'M JUST GOING TO EAT YOU ALL SPRINKLED ON ICE CREAM!

A-A-ANY OTHER IDEAS? NOW'S THE TIME!

I'M JUST GONNA FINISH THIS ICE CREAM FIRST! IT DOESN'T HURT MY TEETH TO EAT IT ANYMORE!

BETELGEUSE'S FINEST
BLORG & JERRY
ICE CREAM
Milky Way Swirl

Y-Y-YOU KNOW WHEN MY MOM AND I WORK OUT TOGETHER, WE DO J-J-JAZZERCISE! MAYBE YOU COULD TRY THAT?

YOU WORK OUT WITH YOUR MOM? REMIND ME TO BEAT YOU UP AFTER HE EATS US!

SEE? THE J-J-JAZZ MUSIC REALLY MAKES THE EXERCISE F-F-FUN!

AAAAAH!

THE END

THE RISE AND FALL OF D'OH!

IAN BOOTHBY STORY

JOHN COSTANZA PENCILS

PHYLLIS NOVIN INKS

ART VILLANUEVA COLORS

KAREN BATES LETTERS

NATHAN KANE EDITOR

MEANWHILE...

KRUSTY! THAT ACTOR YOU PLANTED AS AN *UNDERCOVER KID* AT SPRINGFIELD ELEMENTARY JUST CALLED IN!

THIS COULD BE IMPORTANT. CANCEL MY A.A. MEETING, MY N.A. MEETING, AND MY HEY-HEY MEETING!

HELLO, KRUSTY? A GROUP OF CHILDREN WERE GOING NUTS FOR A MAGAZINE MADE BY SOME KID NAMED BART SIMPSON.

WAIT A SECOND...

HEY, TROY, WHAT'S UP?

THINGS ARE...UM... *RADICAL,* DUDE!

SO KIDS LIKE *MAGAZINES* NOW? DO THEY STILL LIKE JOKES ABOUT *POKEMON*?

I SEE.

MEL, THE OPENING SKETCH IS CUT.

BUT I SPENT *A WEEK* LIVING IN THIS OUTFIT TO GET INTO *CHARACTER!*

LATER...

BART, CAN YOU GET THAT?

DIING DONG!

OKAY, BUT I GET AN EXTRA DESSERT TONIGHT!

LATER, AT KRUSTYLU STUDIOS...

YOU WANT **ME** TO BE ON THE COVER OF YOUR MAGAZINE?

YEP, EVERY MONTH! YOU'VE GOT THAT PERFECT, STUPID, EVERY-MAN LOOK!

WE HAD ONE OF THE **ART MONKEYS** WHIP THIS UP.

D'OH!

EEEP EEEP!

I **KNOW** YOU'VE GOT A NAME. I JUST DON'T WANNA TAKE THE TIME TO LEARN IT!

I CAN'T BELIEVE I GET TO WRITE A MAGAZINE! AND FOR KRUSTY THE CLOWN!

AND **I** CAN'T BELIEVE CHILD LABOR LAWS DON'T COVER THE MAGAZINE INDUSTRY, SO WE **BOTH** WIN!

WOW, THE COVER OF A MAGAZINE! THE GUYS AT WORK ARE GOING TO HAVE A LOT MORE RESPECT FOR ME NOW!

HERE'S YOUR FIRST ASSIGNMENT, KID! WRITE A PARODY OF THE NEW **RAINIER WOLFCASTLE** SCI-FI MOVIE, **DREAM COP!**

IT'S ABOUT A COP WHO FIGHTS CRIME IN DREAMS!

THEY'RE SHOOTING IT IN SPRINGFIELD. I NEED YOU TO GET ON SET, STEAL THE SCRIPT, THEN MAKE FUN OF IT!

CONSIDER IT DONE!

THE *DREAM BEAVER!* NOOOOO!

GRRR!

UM...EXCUSE ME. I WROTE THIS MOVIE, AND MY SCRIPT CLEARLY SAID THAT HE FIGHTS THE DREAM *WEAVER,* NOT DREAM *BEAVER.* THERE MUST BE A TYPO!

AH YES, THIS IS A *HUGE MISTAKE.* LET ME CORRECT THAT AT ONCE.

THANK YOU!

SOMEONE LET A WRITER ON THE SET! *SECURITY!*

BUT... BUT...

PLOP!

3

WHAT DO YOU *MEAN* I'M ALREADY ON SET? LET ME IN!

SOUNDS LIKE *SOMEONE'S* LOOKING TO GET *TASED!*

ZZZAP!

OH, BABY! THIS THING IS GONNA WRITE ITSELF!

SOON...

D'OH!

HOW BAD IS THIS MOVIE? DAM BAD!

HERE IT IS, HOT OFF THE PRESSES AND BEFORE THE FILM IS EVEN OUT! NICE WORK, KID!

I FORGOT TO ASK HOW MUCH I GET PAID!

THAT'S OKAY. I FORGOT TO *PAY* YOU!

SO WHEN ARE YOU GOING TO BRING IN SOME OTHER WRITERS?

A QUARTER PAST *NEVER!* NOW GET BACK TO WORK! YOU'VE GOT THREE MORE MOVIE SETS TO VISIT AND DOZENS MORE PAGES TO WRITE!

≅SIGH!≅

A FEW DAYS LATER, AT THE SPRINGFIELD NUCLEAR POWER PLANT...

"*HOT COCOA FRIDAY*" IS MY FAVORITE DAY OF THE WEEK!

AND *SOME* PEOPLE SAID MR. BURNS SHOULDN'T BE GIVING US FREE HOT COCOA!

I JUST SAID MAYBE THE MONEY SHOULD GO TO *BETTER SHIELDING!*

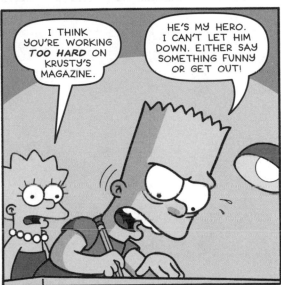

AND SO...

HEY, BART! WHAT WAS WITH THE FOLD-IN JOKE THIS MONTH?

WAS THERE A PROBLEM?

THE FOLDS WERE SO COMPLICATED ONLY THE GUY DELIVERING MY JAPANESE FOOD GOT THE GAG!

I USED TO BE AN ORIGAMI TEACHER.

THE PUNCHLINE IS "NO, YOU GET DOWN OFF A DUCK." HILARIOUS!

KRUSTY, I DON'T THINK I CAN DO A MONTHLY MAGAZINE BY MYSELF ANYMORE.

WELL, GOOD NEWS! YOU DON'T HAVE TO!

REALLY?

YEP, WE'RE GOING WEEKLY!

WHAT'S WRONG, BOY? DIDN'T THE CLOWN MAN LIKE YOUR JOKES?

YEAH...*TOO* MUCH. NO ONE TOLD ME BEING *GOOD* AT SOMETHING MEANT YOU'D HAVE TO WORK EVEN HARDER!

LOOK, DADDY... IT'S THE STUPID FACE MAN FROM THE MAGAZINE!

YES, IT IS, WHICH MEANS IT'S OKAY TO POINT AND LAUGH AT HIM, RALPHIE.

HYUK! I FEELS LIKE I IS YOUR SOCIETAL BETTER!

D'OH!

¿AHEM!¿

AW... HERE YOU GO.

THAT DOES IT! I CAN TAKE LOSING WHAT LITTLE DIGNITY I HAD, BUT NOBODY IS GOING TO MAKE MY SON WORK HARD!

ZZZZ!

KRUSTY, WE QUI--

OH GOOD. I'M GLAD YOU'RE BOTH HERE! YOU'RE FIRED!

WHAT?! WE ARE?

YEAH, I JUST GOT THE CALL! SALES HAVE BOTTOMED OUT. D'OH IS OFFICIALLY D'EAD.

THE FUNERAL'S THIS AFTERNOON. CAN I GET A LIFT?

A WORD FROM THE PUBLISHER...

Welcome to **D'oh! Magazine**, another **High-Kuality*** Krusty Product! You're gonna love it! We've got parodies, spoofs, goofs, and plenty of **madness** from our crack writing staff!

Here's the script for this issue. I changed all the famous people into people I know so you won't get sued. Can I sleep now?

Only if you've learned how to write in your sleep!

⫶GROAN!⫶

That's a groan of **happiness**, folks!

And remember...this is a **totally original idea** and not a rip-off of any other popular magazine!

And if you don't believe that, well...what, me worry?

D'oh! Magazine
Published By KrustyCo, Inc.
A Subsidiary of HK Rustofski Offshore Holdings Limited

Written by	Pencils and Inks by	Colors by	Letters by	Editor
Bart Simpson with Ian Boothby	**James Lloyd**	**Art Villanueva**	**Karen Bates**	**Nathan Kane**

Cover by Jason Ho and Nathan Kane

IAN BOOTHBY
STORY

JAMES LLOYD
ART

NATHAN HAMILL
COLORS

KAREN BATES
LETTERS

NATHAN KANE
EDITOR

THE SOUND AND THE FUNNY

SYNCHRONICITY FOR TWO

NATHAN KANE
STORY

JOHN DELANEY
PENCILS

ANDREW PEPOY
INKS

NATHAN HAMILL
COLORS

KAREN BATES
LETTERS

THE END

WHAT THE HOLE?!

DAVID SEIDMAN
SCRIPT

MIKE KAZALEH
PENCILS & INKS

NATHAN HAMILL
COLORS

KAREN BATES
LETTERS

NATHAN KANE
EDITOR

THE END

NERDS OF PREY

OH NO! BARTMAN'S MYFACE WEB PAGE!

HE'S CHANGED HIS STATUS TO "KIDNAPPED!"

STATUS : KIDNAPPED

BARTMAN

SQUISHEE

I'VE GOT TO HELP HIM!

OW!

BUT I TWISTED MY ANKLE PLAYING FIELD HOCKEY!

LOOKS LIKE I'M STUCK IN THIS CHAIR, BUT MAYBE I CAN SEND OUT AN ANONYMOUS MESSAGE AND SEE IF ANY WOULD-BE HEROES REPLY!

IAN BOOTHBY
SCRIPT

JAMES LLOYD
PENCILS

ANDREW PEPOY
INKS

ART VILLANUEVA
COLORS

KAREN BATES
LETTERS

NATHAN KANE
EDITOR

*NOOOOOOOO!

THE END

MAX DAVISON
WRITER

NINA MATSUMOTO
PENCILS

ANDREW PEPOY
INKS

ART VILLANUEVA
COLORS

KAREN BATES
LETTERS

NATHAN KANE
EDITOR

MOE, YOU CAN'T DO THIS! YOU HAVE TO LET ME BACK IN!

FORGET IT!

I BEEN CHEATED, TREATED LIKE DIRT, AND *LITERALLY* STABBED IN THE BACK WITH A RUSTY SPORK.

BUT AIN'T *NONE OF THAT* COMPARES TO WHAT YOU DID!

"SO THERE I WAS. KICKED OUT OF MY FAVORITE BAR. ALONE. HUNGRY. WITHOUT A FRIEND. DID I MENTION I WAS HUNGRY?"

HIT THE ROAD, RUMMY!

"MY MIND WAS STILL SPINNING FROM WHAT JUST HAPPENED, BUT I TRIED TO REMEMBER HOW THIS STARTED..."

WHISPER!

GOSSIP!

"AND I THINK IT WAS ALL BECAUSE OF *STUPID FLANDERS*..."

ONE WEEK AGO...

KNOCK! KNOCK!

I DON'T WANT TO IMPOSE ON HOMER, BUT ROD AND TODD ARE RIGHT. I *DO* NEED SOME NEW FRIENDS!

KNOW WHAT? YOU'RE TAKIN' SO LONG THAT I'LL JUST POUR YOU THE HOUSE SPECIALTY.

PSSHT!

{SPFFT!}

WHAT IS THIS?

WATERED-DOWN *DUFF!* DON'T MESS WITH THE CLASSICS, I ALWAYS SAY.

I'M SORRY TO BE SO *BLUNT*, BUT THIS BAR IS DIRTY, DISGUSTING, AND *YOU*, SIR, ARE *RUDE!*

THIS PLACE IS... *SUBPAR!*

{GASP!}

SPRINGFIELD

HOW DARE THIS GUY *BAD MOUTH* MY BAR! I RUN A CLASSY JOINT, HERE! TELL HIM, GUYS!

HE'S GOT A POINT, MOE. THIS PLACE *COULD* USE SOME SPRUCING UP.

ISOTOPES

YEAH, THE MUGS ARE ALWAYS DIRTY.

THE WAR BETWEEN THE BATHROOM ROACHES AND RATS MAKES IT *IMPOSSIBLE* TO EVER USE THE JOHN!

AND THIS BEER IS SO BAD, I HAVE TO CHUG IT DOWN! {BRAAP!}

AH, WHAT DO YOU DOPES KNOW? THEM THINGS GIVE THIS PLACE CHARACTER.

WHAT ARE YOU GONNA DO ABOUT IT, CHARLIE CHURCH?

THE NEXT DAY...

IT'D BE NICE IF YOU PUT IN SOME *EFFORT* TO REALLY MAKE THIS PLACE DECENT.

HEY, I FEEL THE SAME WAY ABOUT MY BAR AS I DO ABOUT AMERICA...TAKE IT OR LEAVE IT.

U-S-A! U-S-A!

THOSE BUMS ARE DITCHIN' 'CAUSE THEY DON'T FEEL APPRECIATED? I SHOULD BASH THEIR SKULLS IN!

BUT I PROMISE YOU, *THEY'LL BE BACK*...

DAYS LATER...

THEY NEVER CAME BACK! NED'S STEALIN' ALL MY BUSINESS, HOMER!

I NEED TO SEE WHAT HE'S UP TO. THAT WAY I CAN ONE-UP *HIM!*

WHAT I NEED IS SOME *INSIDE* INFORMATION ABOUT NED'S SET-UP...

SOON...

NED, THAT *NEW BATHROOM ATTENDANT* IS A BIT *ODD*, DON'T YOU THINK?

BATHROOM ATTENDANT?

LET'S SEE IF I REMEMBER MY *BARTENDING COLLEGE* SKILLS. I USED TO BE QUITE THE OL' BOTTLE FLIPPER BACK IN THE DAY...

FWING!

LOOKS LIKE I STILL GOT--

SMASH!

AW, NUTS...

AHHHHHHH!

EVERYONE RUN! IT'S RAINING GLASS! IT'S LIKE ACID RAIN WITH JAGGED EDGES!

LET'S GO TO NED'S!

MEANWHILE, AT NED'S...

IT'S HANS MOLEMAN'S BIRTHDAY, SO IN ADDITION TO OUR HAWAIIAN NIGHT, THERE'S *FREE PIE* FOR EVERYONE!

BUT IT'S ONLY MY *FIRST TIME* IN HERE!

WELL, SIR, THAT MAKES YOU FAMILY!

GREAT PARTY, NED! AND THIS *NEW* BEER IS DE-DIDDLY-LIGHTFUL!

WHY, THANK YOU KINDLY, HOMER! IT'S MY OKTOBERFEST EDITION!

THE NEXT DAY...

HOMER, YOU NEVER SHOWED UP TO GIVE ME LAST NIGHT'S SUPPLY OF SECRETS 'N' GOSSIP!

SORRY, BUT NED THREW THIS *GREAT* PARTY!

AND THEN THERE WAS TRIVIA. LENNY AND I CAME UP WITH A GREAT TEAM NAME, "RISKY QUIZ-NESS!" AND WE WOULD'VE WON IF--

I DON'T CARE, HOMER! I JUST WANT MY INTEL!

REMEMBER WHERE YOUR LOYALTIES LIE! YOU'RE ONE OF *MY* GUYS! I'M THE ONE WHO'S THERE FOR YOU.

REALLY? WHEN WAS THE LAST TIME YOU EVER LISTENED TO *MY* PROBLEMS?

AH, I DON'T GOT TIME FOR YOUR BALONEY! I JUST NEED TA' FIGURE OUT A WAY WE CAN *STOP NED!*

LATER...

HEY, HOMER? I WANT YOU TO TAKE A SPECIAL LOOK AT THE MENU...

THE NEXT DAY...

OKAY, HOMER. I'VE GOT IT! FINALLY FIGURED OUT A WAY TO END NED'S REIGN OF TERROR!

FROM WHAT YOU'VE TOLD ME, NED'S BAR IS WORKIN' BECAUSE HE'S HAPPY AND CREATES A WELCOMING ENVIRONMENT.

SO YOU'RE GOING TO DO THAT WITH YOUR OWN BAR?

HECK NO! I'M GOING TO UNLEASH THESE HUNGRY *RACCOONS* INTO THE AIR DUCTS AND RUIN HIS BAR FOREVER!

GROWL!

SNARL!

BITE!

BWA-HA-HA!

AND THEN THEY'LL ALL COME RUNNIN' BACK TO MOE! MY PLAN IS PERFECT!

HISS!

;GULP!;

NED? I HAVE TO TELL YOU SOMETHING...

...AND THEN THE ONE RACCOON STARED RIGHT AT ME AND THREATENED MY LIFE WITH HIS EYES!

WOW! MOE REALLY MEANS BUSINESS.

THANKS FOR TELLING ME, HOMER. IT MEANS A LOT.

AWWW. SWEET, DOOMED FLANDERS.

THANKFULLY I'VE *ALREADY* PROTECTED THIS PLACE AGAINST RACCOONS.

HUH? YOU HAVE?

YESIREE! THE BIBLE MENTIONS SOMETHING ABOUT RACCOONS AND THEIR ILK BEING UNCLEAN CREATURES*, SO I TAKE EXTRA PRECAUTIONS AGAINST THEM! IF THE GOOD BOOK SAYS IT, I'LL DO IT!

UMM... OKAY...

RACCOON B-GONE

*EDITOR'S BOX: I BELIEVE NED'S REFERRING TO LEVITICUS, CHAPTER 11-SO SAYETH THE EDITOR

THAT RAT LET THE CAT OUT OF THE BAG ABOUT THE RACOONS! MY MOLE IS A *TWO-FACED WEASEL!*

NED

I KNOW IT WAS *YOU*, HOMER. YOU BROKE MY HEART.

HUH?

I SAW YOU TALKIN' TO NED. HOW COULD YOU? THAT HURTS!

YOU KNOW WHAT? IT HURTS *EVERYONE ELSE* HOW YOU TREAT THEM! NED TREATS US LIKE HUMAN BEINGS!

I WAS YOUR LAST FRIEND, AND YOU NEVER ONCE THANKED ME! YOU JUST DECIDED TO USE ME AS A SPY! WELL, NO MORE! YOU CAN USE YOUR *RACCOONS* AS SPIES NOW!

ACTUALLY, DON'T. THEY'LL PROBABLY RIP NED'S PLACE APART...

WHY I OUGHTTA--

AW, WHO AM I KIDDING? YOU'RE RIGHT, HOMER. I *DO* TAKE YOU GUYS FOR GRANTED... LIKE RUNNING WATER OR PENICILLIN. I NEED TO CHANGE.

YOU MEAN IT? HOW ABOUT START BY USING CLEAN BEER MUGS?

URGH. THAT SOUNDS *EXCESSIVE,* BUT I'LL DO IT.

BUT IF THINGS DON'T CHANGE SOON, MOE'S WILL GO OUT OF BUSINESS! HOW CAN WE CONVINCE NED TO CLOSE HIS BAR?

I MIGHT HAVE ONE *LAST BIT* OF INSIDE INFO...

NED, I'M GOING TO MISS THIS PLACE!

DON'T WORRY. A HIGHER POWER SAYS THAT EVERYTHING WILL BE BETTER NOW!

WELCOME BACK, BOYS. MOE'S BEEN *WAITIN'* FOR YOU...

SOON...

I'VE BEEN WAITIN' FOR YOU SO'S I COULD APOLOGIZE. I AIN'T BEEN TREATING YOU WITH RESPECT AND AFFECTION AND WHADDYA CALL IT... *COMMON HUMAN DECENCY*. THAT'S ALL GONNA CHANGE.

YOU GOT A PROBLEM? I'LL LISTEN. EVEN IF IT'S PAINFULLY BORING AND MAKES ME WANT TO RIP OFF MY EARS WITH A HACKSAW.

AND BEFORE FLANDERS WENT OUT OF BUSINESS, I BOUGHT UP ALL HIS REMAINING MICROBREWS.

WOO-HOO!

I'VE GOT A KEG FULL OF "HOMERBRAU" HERE!

FLANDERS ALE

THE END

STRETCH BOB and SIDESHOW CLOBBER!

...AND THANKS TO OUR SURPRISE GUESTS, *STRETCH DUDE* AND *CLOBBER GIRL*, WHO STOPPED SIDESHOW BOB FROM BLOWING UP THE STUDIO!

BECAUSE OF THEM, THE ONLY *BOMB* ON THE SHOW TODAY WAS THE MONKEY *"MAD MEN"* SKETCH!

OOF!

POW!

OOK! AK!

MATT GROENING

KRACK!

THAT SOUNDED LIKE HIS *FUNNY BONE!* HA!

COULD YOU *PLEASE* TURN OFF THAT INFERNAL TELEVISION? OR AT LEAST CHANGE THE CHANNEL TO PBS!?

WHAT'D YOU SAY, BOB? I WAS READING THIS STRETCH DUDE AND CLOBBER GIRL *COMIC BOOK!*

SINCE THEY'RE REAL, THEY'RE *PUBLIC DOMAIN,* AND THOSE BONGO COMICS FOLKS'LL PUBLISH *ANYTHING* THEY DON'T HAVE TO PAY THE RIGHTS FOR!

IAN BOOTHBY
SCRIPT

JOHN DELANEY
PENCILS

ANDREW PEPOY
INKS

ART VILLANUEVA
COLORS

KAREN BATES
LETTERS

NATHAN KANE
EDITOR

WANT TO READ THE LATEST ISSUE OF *"THE WALKING NED"*?

THE WALKING NED

NO! WHAT I DESIRE IS *SWEET REVENGE!*

WELL, YOU'LL NEVER BEAT STRETCH DUDE AND CLOBBER GIRL. SEE HERE...IT SHOWS THEM GETTING THEIR AMAZING POWERS AFTER BEING OVEREXPOSED TO *X-RAYS!*

HI, EVERYBODY!

HI, DOCTOR NICK!

TIME FOR YOUR X-RAY, MR. SIDESHOW! LET'S SEE HOW YOUR *BODY BONES* ARE DOING BEFORE THEY TAKE YOU OFF TO JAIL!

DR. NICK, WOULD YOU MIND TURNING THE X-RAY MACHINE UP TO DANGEROUS LEVELS?

THAT'S SUPER UNETHICAL.

BUT I NEED TO FILM *SOMETHING* FOR THE *HOSPITAL PARTY BLOOPER REEL,* SO OKAY!

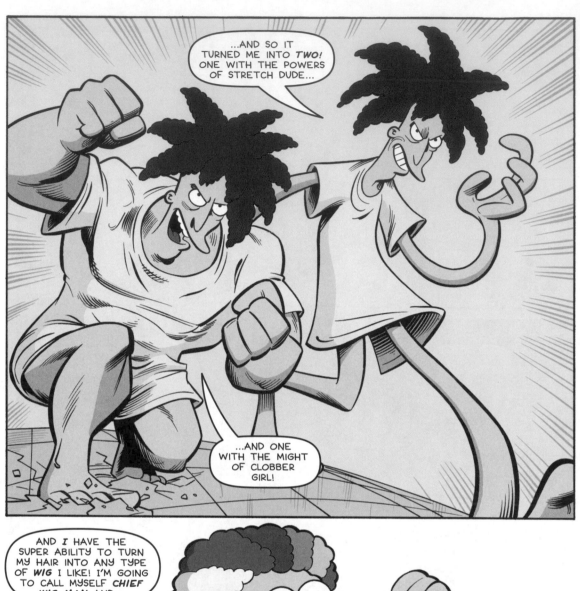
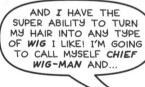

PEOPLE OF SPRINGFIELD! YOUR HEROES ARE NOW A *TETHERBALL!*

WHACK!

OW!

QUIT IT!

AND WITHOUT THEM TO PROTECT YOU, WE DECLARE *OURSELVES* YOUR NEW OVERLORDS!

AS THE MAYOR, I...ER, AH...GIVE IN TO ALL YOUR DEMANDS!

WHAT? COME ON!

VOTE FOR ME AND I'LL GIVE IN TO ALL YOUR DEMANDS!

IT'S THE PLATFORM I RAN ON!

OH YEAH, THAT'S RIGHT. I ONLY VOTED FOR YOU 'CAUSE THE OTHER GUY WANTED TO PUT BIKE LANES ON THE STREETS!

SO WHAT IS IT YOU TWO BOBS WANT, EXACTLY?

THE AZTEC MOVIE THEATER HAS TO SHOW CLASSIC FILMS AGAIN, NOT JUST MICHAEL BAY MOVIES THEY TAPED OFF TELEVISION!

I KNEW THEY WUZ DOIN' THAT! REAL MOVIES DON'T HAVE ADS IN THE MIDDLE OF 'EM FOR FOOT FUNGUS CREAM!

THE SPRINGFIELD ORCHESTRA HAS TO LEARN *ACTUAL* SONGS, NOT JUST HIDE THEIR CELL PHONES INSIDE THEIR INSTRUMENTS AND PLAY PRE-RECORDED SONGS DURING CONCERTS.

THAT'S NOT TRUE!

YOU HAVE THREE NEW MESSAGES!

AND THE VEGETARIAN OPTION AT LOCAL RESTAURANTS CAN'T JUST BE TO, "GO SOMEWHERE ELSE BEFORE I CALL A COP!"

YOU KNOW, I ACTUALLY *AGREE* WITH YOUR IDEAS. MAYBE WE COULD WORK SOMETHING OUT!

BUT OUR FIRST ORDER OF BUSINESS WILL BE TO *MURDER* BART SIMPSON.

YOU LOST HER THERE...RIGHT, SIS? SIS?!

I'M THINKING, I'M THINKING!

SORRY, SIDESHOW BOBS, YOU WANT MY BROTHER, YOU'LL HAVE TO GO THROUGH ME!

THAT WAS THE PLAN ALL ALONG. LET'S GET STARTED!

THE MORE *SQUEAMISH* AMONG THE AUDIENCE MIGHT WANT TO LOOK AWAY FOR A FEW MOMENTS!

HOURS LATER...

HEY, THIS IS TAKING A WHILE! WOULD YOU FELLAS LIKE TO BUY SOME *DONUTS* TO SPEED THINGS UP?*

KRUSTY BURGER

BIFF!

WHAM!

LARD LAD DONUTS

*YOU 'SIMPSONS TAPPED OUT' PLAYERS KNOW WHAT GIL'S SAYIN'!—EDITOR NATHAN

:PANT!:

HEY, GUYS!

:WHEEZE!:

HOW DID YOU GET FREE?

YOU USED A SHEET BEND AND A CLOVE HITCH KNOT. PRETTY EASY TO UNTIE FOR ANYONE WITH EVEN BASIC GIRL SCOUT TRAINING.

YOU STILL CAN'T BEAT US! WE'RE *ADULTS!*

YEAH, ADULTS THAT HAVE *EXHAUSTED THEMSELVES* BY FIGHTING WITH EACH OTHER.

A FEW SECONDS LATER...

AND SO THE DAY IS SAVED BECAUSE BROTHERS ARE JERKS WHO CAN'T SHARE!

HEY, I THINK I'M OFFENDED BY THAT!

THE END!

BRIT SIMPSON!

IAN BOOTHBY
WRITER

JOHN DELANEY
PENCILS

ANDREW PEPOY
INKS

ART VILLANUEVA
COLORS

KAREN BATES
LETTERS

NATHAN KANE
EDITOR

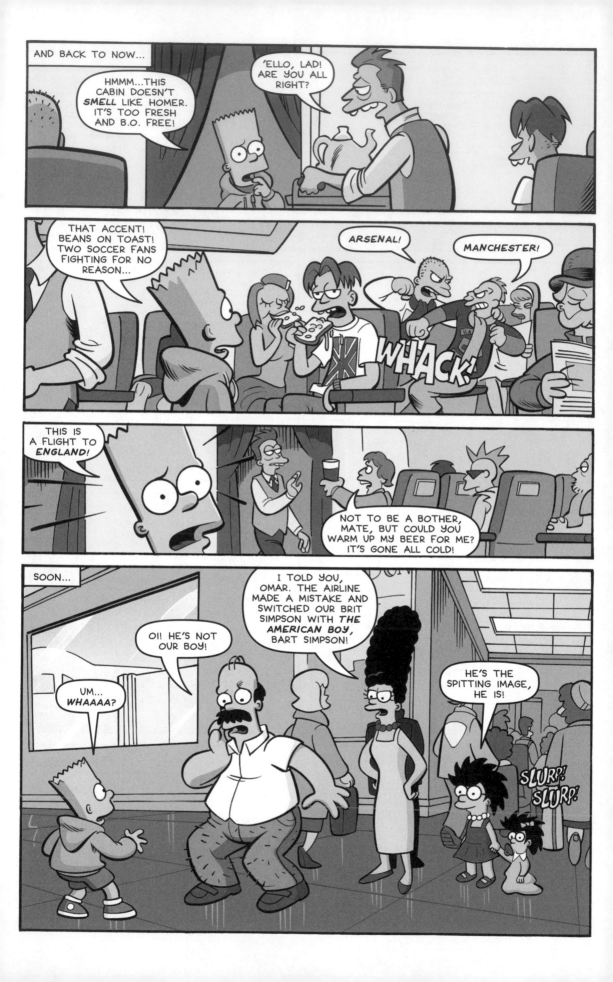

HELLO, MR. BUMBLE. HELLO, MR. SMITTERS.

HELLO, EMPLOYEE! GET BACK TO WORK!

AH...WE'RE USING *CHILD LABOUR* AGAIN! EXEMPLARY!

MMM... *SCONES!*

DROOL!

LISTER'S CLOTTED CREAM SCONES
We'll clot your heart!

SO WHAT'S YOUR JOB HERE?

WIND MONITOR!

WHICH MEANS?

YOU SEE THAT WIND OUT THERE?

YEAH.

I MONITOR IT!

IT'S ⫶YAWN!⫶ HARD WORK, BUT *SOMEONE* HAS TO DO IT!

WATCHING THE WIND? AND I THOUGHT *HOMER* HAD A JOB THAT *BLOWS!*

SNXXX!

THAT'S WHAT THEY TEACH YOU IN AMERICA?

ACTUALLY, IN AMERICA THEY TEACH US WE HAVE THE RIGHT TO FREE SPEECH, SO WE CAN JUST MAKE UP THE HISTORY WE WANT!

NOW WHO VOTES TO MAKE MY STORY THE ACTUAL HISTORY OF ENGLAND?

WOOO!

YEAH!

AND *THAT'S* AMERICAN DEMOCRACY IN ACTION!

THAT WAS BRILLIANT! I'VE NEVER SEEN TEACHER TURN THAT SHADE OF PURPLE BEFORE.

WITH THE RIGHT MATERIAL, TEACHERS CAN BE TURNED *ALL* THE COLORS OF THE RAINBOW

HA! GOT YOUR DUMB HAT!

BOING!

WHAT?

STOP IN THE NAME OF THE LAW!

TODAY YOU'VE MADE AN ENEMY OF *SIDESHOW BOBBY*!

OI OI! WELL, THAT WAS *TERRIBLE* AS USUAL!

THIS USED TO BE AN EDUCATIONAL PROGRAM UNTIL THATCHER CUT OUR FUNDING IN THE EIGHTIES!

I DON'T THINK KRUMPET'S HEART'S IN THIS ANYMORE!

TURN OFF THE TELLY! I BEG YOU! END MY SHAME!

IT'S *TEA TIME!*

TEA? *BLECCH!*

OH, THAT'S JUST WHAT WE CALL IT. IT'S ACTUALLY *MILK AND BISCUITS!*

YOU MEAN COOKIES? THEN CALL IT *"COOKIE TIME!"* SHEESH, ENGLAND, LEARN HOW TO MARKET THINGS!

OMAR? WHAT ARE YOU DOING HOME SO EARLY?

THE WIND STOPPED, SO THEY SENT US ALL HOME.

I'M GOING TO WATCH THE FOOTBALL MATCH!

AND IT'S BEEN *THREE HOURS* WITHOUT EITHER TEAM SCORING. I CAN'T REMEMBER A MORE EXCITING MATCH!

OH GOOD! THERE'S STILL A FEW MORE HOURS OF NOTHING HAPPENING TO WATCH!

NO'H!

WHAT HAPPENED?

I COULDN'T AFFORD TO PAY MY TELEVISION LICENCE, AND THEY CUT ME OFF!

¡MOAN!¡ I WISH THERE WAS SOME WAY TO BRING IN A LITTLE MORE MONEY!

YOU CAN STOP GIVING ME AN ALLOWANCE!

THAT'S SWEET, BUT I STOPPED YEARS AGO. I'VE JUST BEEN TAKING ONE OF THE FIVE POUND NOTES YOU'VE BEEN SAVING IN YOUR SOCK DRAWER AND GIVING IT BACK TO YOU EVERY WEEK.

YOU KNOW...BACK IN AMERICA WHEN HOMER NEEDS EXTRA CASH, HE STARTS UP A *GET RICH QUICK SCHEME.*

AND THOSE USUALLY END WELL?

WELL, IT'S BETTER TO JUST JUMP INTO THEM WITHOUT THINKING TOO MUCH.

RIDE THE *WIND WHEEL!*

ENJOY FRESHLY SPUN COTTON CANDY!

THAT'S OKAY! NOW YOU KNOW THE *RIGHT* NAME FOR IT!

WE CALL IT "CANDY *FLOSS.*"

AND DON'T FORGET TO VISIT THE *HYPNO-DISC* BEFORE YOU GO!

YOU DON'T WANT TO LEAVE! YOU WANT TO SPEND MORE MONEY!

WE DON'T WANT TO LEAVE...WE WANT TO SPEND MORE MONEY...

AND SO...

YOU'RE *BRILLIANT,* BOY! THE MONEY IS JUST ROLLING IN!

THAT'S GREAT! BUT YOU HAVE TO REMEMBER *ONE THING!*

NO MATTER WHAT, NEVER SAY, "NOTHING CAN POSSIBLY GO WRONG!"

BUT NOTHING *CAN* POSSIBLY GO WRONG!

FINALLY, IN THE MIDDLE OF WESTMINSTER BRIDGE...

I CAN'T MOVE!

SORRY, OMAR. LOOKS LIKE WE'LL BE STUCK LIKE THIS *FOREVER*.

KEEP YOUR CHIN UP, LAD. IT'S LONDON. JUST WAIT FIVE MINUTES.

THERE WE GO! RIGHT AS RAIN, SAYS I!

AT LEAST WE STILL HAVE THE MONEY.

OH, THAT ALL BLEW AWAY IN THE WIND!

I DIDN'T WANT TO TELL YOU, BUT MOST OF HOMER'S SCHEMES USUALLY END THIS WAY, TOO.

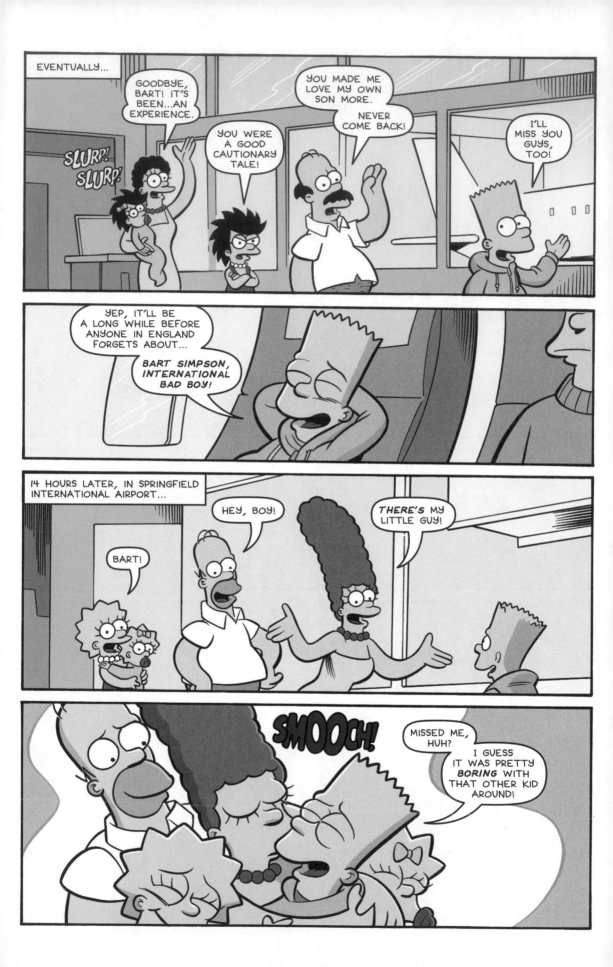

HEH.

WHAT?

WE NEVER KNEW HOW GOOD WE HAD IT WITH YOU, BOY!

BRIT WAS LIKE AN *EARTH-QUAKE* MADE OF MISCHIEF!

IT'S SO GOOD TO HAVE YOU HOME!

RIVALS

ATE 3

UH...WHY DOES THE CAR LOOK LIKE MASHED POTATOES WITH A SAUSAGE IN IT?

P P

BRIT AND I OPENED A *BANGERS AND MASH* FOOD STAND OUT OF MY CAR.

HOW DID IT DO?

GREAT AT FIRST, THEN BARNEY OPENED THE *"EVERYONE'S A WIENER"* FLAME-BROILED HOT DOG WAGON.

BRIT DIDN'T LIKE THE COMPETITION AND REPLACED BARNEY'S HOT DOGS WITH FIRECRACKERS.

IT ALL GOT PRETTY CRAZY AFTER THAT.

THAT SOUNDS AMAZING!

IT WAS NEVER A DULL MOMENT WITH BRIT AROUND!

WHAT TH--?!

RALPH'S ROOM

MATT GROENING

SERGIO ARAGONÈS
STORY & ART

NATHAN HAMILL
COLORS

BILL MORRISON
EDITOR

BUSY HANDS PAPERCRAFT PROJECT!

WHAT YOU WILL NEED:
- Scissors, adhesive tape, and a straight edge (such as a ruler).
- An ability to fold along straight lines.
- An additional "mint condition" copy of this book secured elsewhere!

1. Cut out figures and bases.
2. Cut along the dotted line at the base of each figure and also the center of each curved base. (Be careful not to cut too far!)
3. Connect base to figure as shown (Fig. 1).
4. Before cutting out the shapes, use a ruler and a slightly rounded metal tool (like the edge of a key) to first score, and then fold lightly along all the interior lines (this will make final folds much easier).
5. Cut along the exterior shape. Make sure to cut all the way to where the walls, the roof, and the flap lines meet (Fig. 2).

Fig. 1

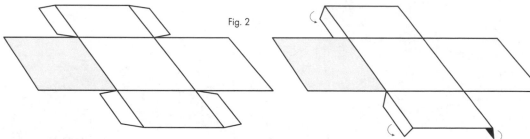

Fig. 2

6. Form building by folding walls into place (Fig. 3) and secure all tabs to the interior of the building with tape (Fig. 4).

Fig. 3

Fig. 4

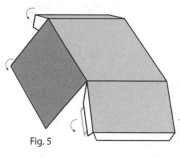

Fig. 5

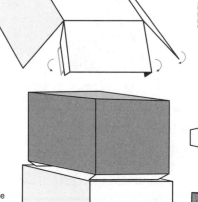

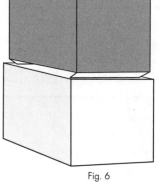

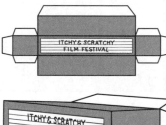

7. Cut and fold second story shape as shown (Fig. 5), and secure with tape. See cutout page for instructions on placement of roof items. Then, place the second story on top of building and secure bottom flaps onto top of first story with tape (Fig. 6).

Fig. 6

Fig. 7

8. Cut and fold marquee into box-like shape as shown (Fig. 7), and secure with tape. Fold down the top rear tab and then fold in the two side tabs, taping them to the rear tab.

9. Fold back the tab on the Aztec sign and tape it to the top of the marquee (Fig. 8)

10. Place a piece of looped tape on the back of the marquee and press it firmly into place on the front of the building (Fig. 9).

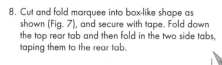

Fig. 8

Fig. 9

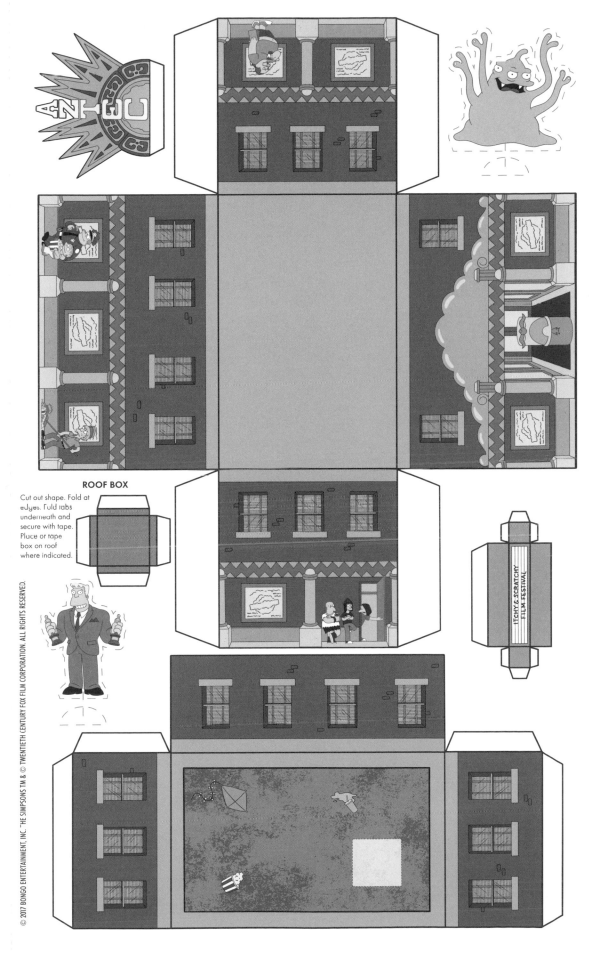

ROOF BOX

Cut out shape. Fold at edges. Fold tabs underneath and secure with tape. Place or tape box on roof where indicated.

ITCHY & SCRATCHY FILM FESTIVAL